PIGGLES' GUIDE TO...

HOT AIR BALLOONS

BY KIRSTY HOLMES

BookLife
PUBLISHING

©2018
BookLife Publishing
King's Lynn
Norfolk PE30 4LS

All rights reserved.
Printed in Malaysia.

A catalogue record for this
book is available from the
British Library.

ISBN: 978-1-78637-495-0

Written by:
Kirsty Holmes

Edited by:
Holly Duhig

Designed by:
Danielle Rippengill

IMAGE CREDITS

All images are courtesy of Shutterstock.com, unless otherwise specified. With thanks to Getty Images, Thinkstock Photo and iStockphoto. Cover – NotionPic, A–R–T, logika600, BiterBig, ringo ringo. 1 – BiterBig. 2 – Iconic Bestiary, NotionPic. 3 – BiterBig. 4 – NotionPic, Vector Tradition, Faber14, Vector A. 5 – Mascha Tace. NotionPic. 6 – Faber14, Vector Tradition, Jemastock. 7 – Faber14, NotionPic, Iyeyee, Julia's Art, Ilyafs. 8 & 9 – BiterBig, Vector Tradition, NotionPic. 10 – BiterBig, MoonRock, Rvector, Nosopyrik, aliaksei kruhlenian, NotionPic. 11 – Iconic Bestiary, NotionPic. 12 – BiterBig, NotionPic. 13 – BiterBig, ringo ringo. 14 & 15 – NotionPic, Vector Tradition, Faber14, Irina Strelnikova. 16 – Vector Tradition, Kirill Galkin. 17 – BiterBig, NotionPic, ringo ringo. 18 – Ilyafs, mckenna71. 20 – Mascha Tace, NotionPic, BiterBig. 21 – BiterBig, NotionPic, ArtMalivanov, DRogatnev, Usagi–P. 22 – aliaksei kruhlenian, lukpedclub, BiterBig. 23 – NotionPic, Vector Tradition. 24 – BiterBig.

CONTENTS

PAGE 4 — Welcome to Flight School!

PAGE 6 — Lesson 1: What Is a Hot Air Balloon?

PAGE 8 — Lesson 2: Parts of a Hot Air Balloon

PAGE 10 — Lesson 3: Inside a Hot Air Balloon

PAGE 12 — Lesson 4: Lift!

PAGE 14 — Lesson 5: Navigation!

PAGE 16 — Lesson 6: Launching and Landing

PAGE 18 — Lesson 7: Famous Hot Air Balloons

PAGE 20 — Flight Check

PAGE 22 — Bonus Lesson: Bungee!

PAGE 24 — Glossary and Index

WORDS THAT LOOK LIKE <u>this</u> CAN BE FOUND IN THE GLOSSARY ON PAGE 24.

WELCOME TO FLIGHT SCHOOL!

So you're interested in hot air balloons? Do you dream of floating through the air in a giant basket? Then you've come to the right place! The Sty in the Sky Flight School!

STY IN THE SKY
ACADEMY

EARN YOUR WINGS

Here, you will learn all you need to know about some amazing flying machines, and join the **<u>elite</u>** flying force known as the Pink Wings! So pay attention: it's time to FLY!

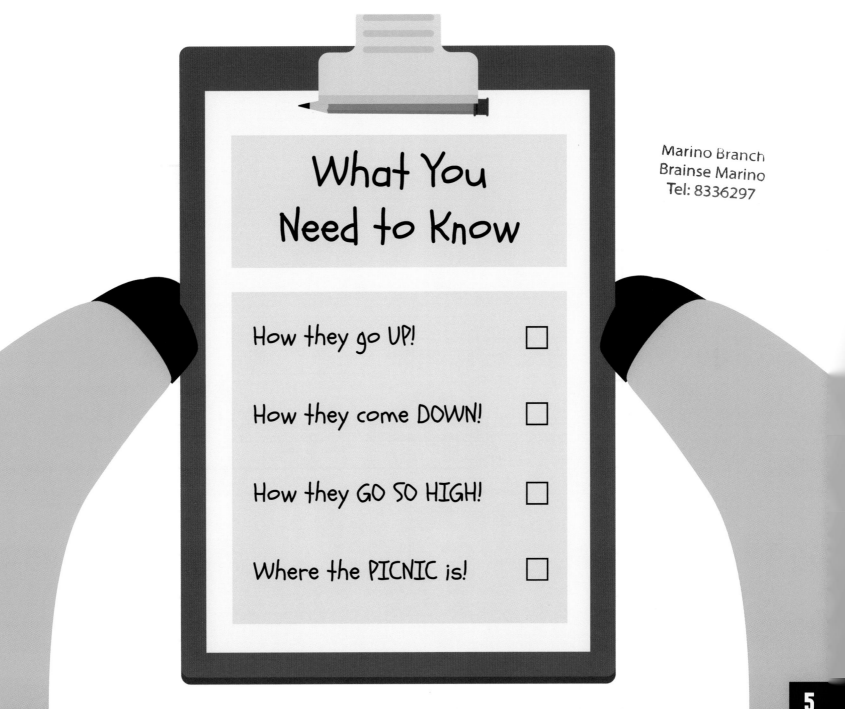

What You Need to Know

How they go UP! ☐

How they come DOWN! ☐

How they GO SO HIGH! ☐

Where the PICNIC is! ☐

Marino Branch
Brainse Marino
Tel: 8336297

Hot air balloons are a type of lighter-than-air (LTA) aircraft.

This means they are flying machines that weigh less than the air around them, making them float.

Hot air balloons are used to carry passengers.
They are usually only big enough for a few passengers.

Now then class; who can tell me how many different balloons there are here today?

LESSON 2:

PARTS OF A
HOT AIR BALLOON

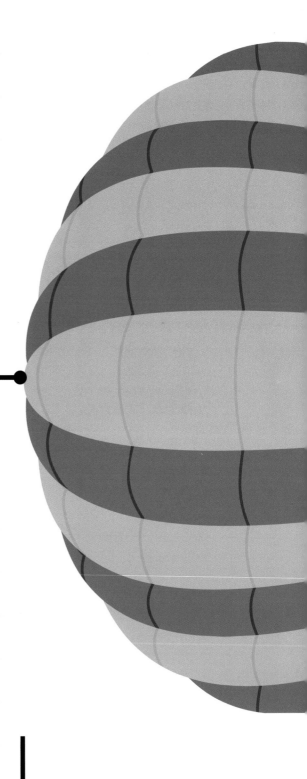

VALVE

This allows the pilot to let air out of the balloon.

ENVELOPE

Hot air balloons all feature a large bag made from <u>nylon</u> to lift the balloon into the air.

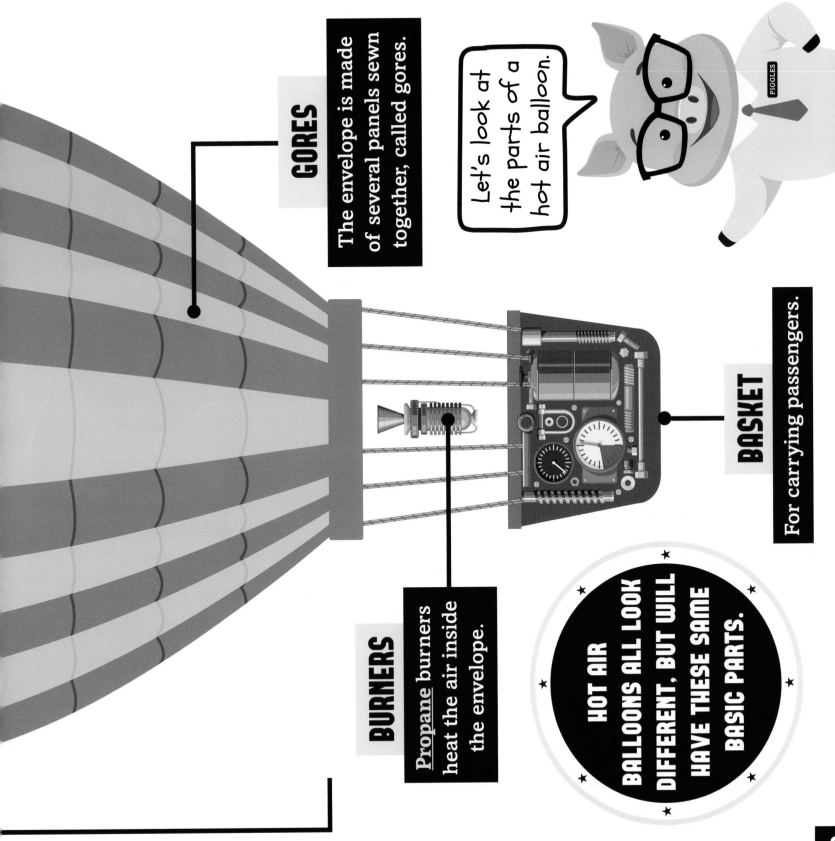

GORES

The envelope is made of several panels sewn together, called gores.

Let's look at the parts of a hot air balloon.

PIGGLES

BASKET

For carrying passengers.

BURNERS

Propane burners heat the air inside the envelope.

HOT AIR BALLOONS ALL LOOK DIFFERENT, BUT WILL HAVE THESE SAME BASIC PARTS.

Lesson 3:
INSIDE A HOT AIR BALLOON

THERMOMETER
Shows Air Temperature

PROPANE TANKS
Fuel

COMPASS
Shows Direction

ALTIMETER
Shows Height

PILOT
Piggles

PICNIC
Very Important

The basket holds tanks of propane gas to fuel the burners, and also holds **instruments** the pilot needs. Hot air balloon baskets are usually made of **wicker** and are very light.

The passengers also travel in the basket with the pilot.
There aren't any seats, doors or stairs. Passengers have to climb in, and stand for the whole trip. Don't worry – the views are amazing!

LESSON 4:

LIFT!

To get a hot air balloon into the sky, you need to create lift. Lift is the **force** which pushes an aircraft upwards. Hot air balloons use hot and cold air to create lift.

USE THIS SIMPLE RULE:

HOT AIR
Rises Up

COLD AIR
Sinks Down

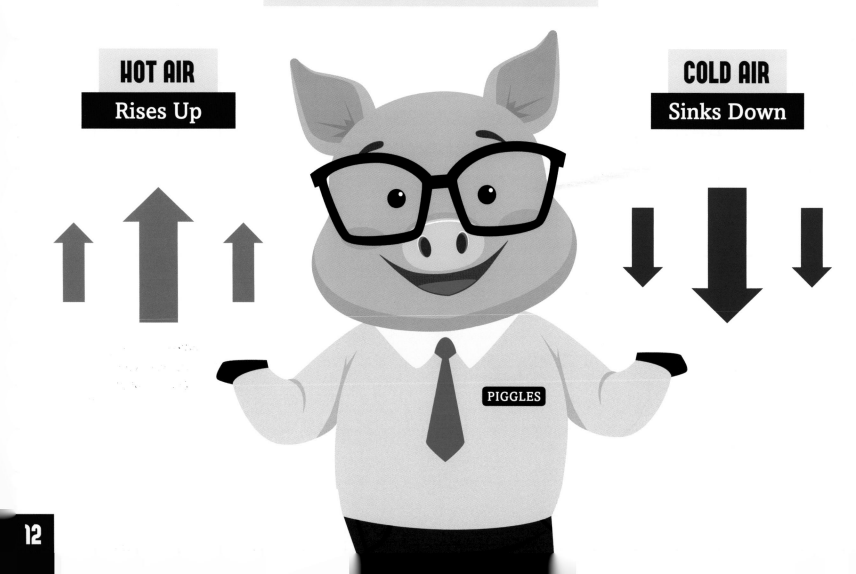

PIGGLES

The pilot uses the burners to heat the air inside the envelope.

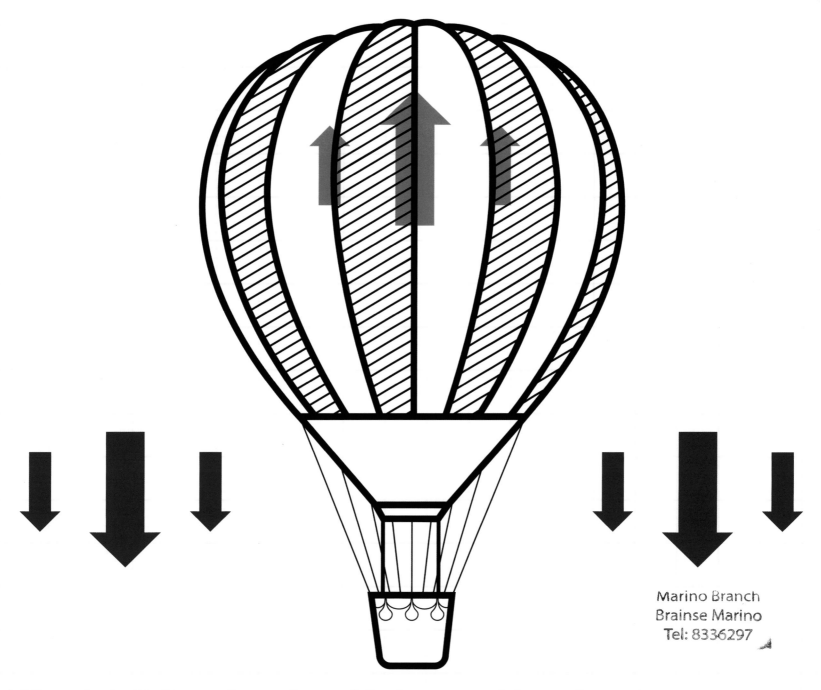

Hot air is lighter than the cold air around it, and so rises up, taking the balloon with it!

NAVIGATION!

Pilots don't have much control over where the balloon goes.
The wind will push the balloon along instead as it is so light.

To control the direction, the pilot can change **altitude** and try and catch the wind going in the right direction.

PILOTS USE A QUIET LIQUID BURNER, CALLED A WHISPER BURNER, OVER FIELDS SO THEY DON'T SCARE THE ANIMALS.

STY IN THE SKY
ACADEMY
EARN YOUR WINGS

Often a crew will follow the balloon in a car to see where it lands and pick up the passengers.

LESSON 6:
LAUNCHING AND LANDING

Getting into the air is called 'launching'. The crew attach the burner to the basket, then the envelope, then lay it on the ground. The burner blasts hot air, filling the balloon.

At the end of a flight, the pilot opens the top of the balloon and slowly lets out the heat, so the balloon gets lower. Good landing sites have wide open spaces, and no power lines.

The pilot will bump the balloon gently along the ground until it stops.

LESSON 7:
FAMOUS HOT AIR BALLOONS

VIJAYPAT SINGHANIA

In 2005, Vijaypat Singhania set the world record for the highest altitude flight in a hot air balloon. He flew to 6,614 metres (m) above India.

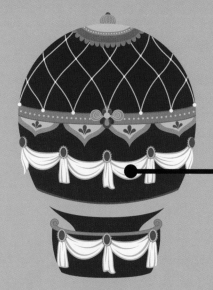

MONTGOLFIER BROTHERS

The Montgolfier Brothers flew the first hot air balloon ever, for King Louis XVI in 1783. Its passengers were a duck, a sheep and a rooster!

DOUBLE EAGLE II

In 1978, Ben Abruzzo, Maxie Anderson and Larry Newman successfully crossed the Atlantic Ocean in a hot air balloon – the first time this had been achieved!

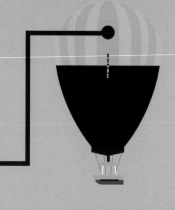

FIRST BALLOON TO FLY AROUND THE WORLD

BREITLING
ORBITER 3

BREITLING ORBITER 3

The first balloon to fly all the way around the world was the Breitling Orbiter 3, piloted by Bertrand Piccard and Brian Jones.

FLIGHT CHECK

OK, students. Let's test your knowledge about hot air balloons and see if you've been paying attention! Get them all right, and you earn your Pink Wings!

Questions

1. What is the correct name for the inflated part of the balloon?

2. What fuel does the burner use?

3. What passengers were in the first ever balloon flight?

4. Which goes up – hot air, or cold air?

5. What is the proper word for 'getting up in the air'?

Did you get all the answers right? You did? Well done!

This means you are now an expert **aviator** and you have become a member of the world's most elite flying force: The Pink Wings!

BUNGEE!

Pilots have to learn all about balloons and spend many years learning to fly them safely. They have to know how to launch and land, and what to do in an emergency...

STEP ONE
Identify Emergency

"WE'VE EATEN ALL THE PICNIC FOOD!"

STEP TWO
Don't Panic

STEP THREE
Grab Bungee

GLOSSARY

ALTITUDE — height of an aircraft from the ground

AVIATOR — someone who flies an aircraft

ELITE — someone or something which is the best of a group

FORCE — a power or energy

INSTRUMENTS — a tool or device for doing a job

NYLON — a silky fabric made of plastic

PROPANE — a flammable gas used as fuel

WICKER — a basket made out of branches that are weaved together

INDEX

BASKET 4, 9–11, 16

BURNERS 9–10, 13, 15–16, 20

ENVELOPE 8–9, 13, 16

FORCES 12

INSTRUMENTS 10

MONTGOLFIER BROTHERS 18

PASSENGERS 7, 9, 11, 15, 18, 20